SCHOOL
THEN AND NOW

by Robin Nelson

Lerner Publications · Minneapolis

Learning About Seeds
We planted our seeds on Wed. April 26th
We have been growing our garden for this many days:

We go to **school** to learn and see friends.

School has changed
over time.

Long ago, children had to walk many miles to school.

Now, children take buses
to school.

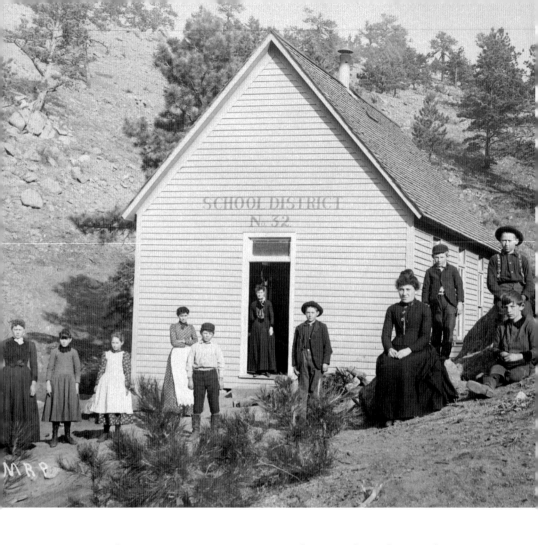

Long ago, schools had only one room.

Now, schools are large
buildings with many rooms.

Long ago, children in your
class were many ages.

Now, children in your class
are all the same age.

Long ago, students had to share a desk.

Now, students have their own desks.

Long ago, students wrote on **slates**.

Now, students write
in notebooks.

Long ago, students wrote with **chalk**.

Now, students write
with pencils.

Long ago, students learned
reading, writing, and **arithmetic**.

Now, students also learn
science and social studies.

Schools Timeline

1635
First public
school opens.

1565
Pencil is invented.

1636
Harvard, the first
college, is started.

1828
Noah Webster
publishes his
first dictionary.

1882
Fountain pen
is invented.

1873
First public
kindergarten
opens.

1900
Paper clip
is invented.

1658
First children's picture book is published.

1731
First public library opens.

1708
First illustrated history book is published.

1821
First public high school opens.

1903
Crayola crayon is invented.

1939
School buses are painted yellow.

1938
Ballpoint pen is invented.

1943
Computer is invented.

School Facts

 The first teachers in America were men. Most of these teachers started teaching at 16 years old.

 From 1775 to 1783, there was a war going on in America. During this time, many schools were closed because the teachers were fighting in the army.

 Long ago, some schools had paper windows instead of glass.

Paper was expensive in colonial times. Students sometimes wrote on tree bark instead.

 In many pioneer towns, the schoolhouse was also used as the church.

 Teachers were very strict. If a student did not learn their lesson, they had to wear a dunce hat. They put on the tall, pointy hat and sat at the front of the classroom. This would embarrass the student.

Glossary

 arithmetic – math, using numbers

 chalk – material used for writing on a blackboard

 school – a place where students learn from teachers

 science – what people know about the world and the things that are in it

 slates – small blackboards

Index

Lerner Publications Company
A division of Lerner Publishing Group, Inc.
241 First Avenue North
Minneapolis, MN 55401 USA

For reading levels and more information, look up this title at www.lernerbooks.com.

Library of Congress Cataloging-in-Publication Data

Nelson, Robin, 1971–
　　School then and now / by Robin Nelson.
　　　　p.　cm. — (First step nonfiction)
　　Includes index.
　　Summary: Briefly describes how school in the United States has changed through the years, including such topics as transportation, supplies, and subjects taught.
　　ISBN-13: 978–0–8225–4640–5 (lib. bdg. : alk. paper)
　　ISBN-10: 0–8225–4640–X (lib. bdg. : alk. paper)
　　1. Schools—United States—Juvenile literature. [1. Schools—History.] I. Title. II. Series.
LA205 .N45　2003
371'.00973—dc21   2002010680

Manufactured in the United States of America
11 – CG – 12/1/14